StarBuilder
Inspirations

by *Laura Murray*

Acknowledgements

With thanks to my husband and best friend, Jim,
for his unconditional support, love, and numerous contributions to this book,
including painting hundreds of StarBuilder shapes.
To Shelly Stokes for her generous sharing of expertise, including excerpts
from her book "Paintstiks on Fabric".
To Susan Stein for her encouragement and insight.
To Sharon Boerbon Hanson for her guidance throughout the entire process
and her much needed editorial support.
To Karen Sheahan for her patience and exceptional graphic design talents.

© 2009, Laura J. Murray

Published and Distributed by:

Laura Murray Designs

5021 15th Ave S,Mpls, MN 55417 U.S.A.

612-825-1209

www.lauramurraydesigns.com

Photography by Laura Murray and Shelly Stokes.
Cover Photography by Petronella Ytsma
Edited by Sharon Boerbon Hanson
Cover Design /Book Design by Karen Sheahan

ISBN-10: 0-615-30819-8

ISBN-13: 978-0-615-30819-7

Printed and bound in the United States of America

Table of Contents

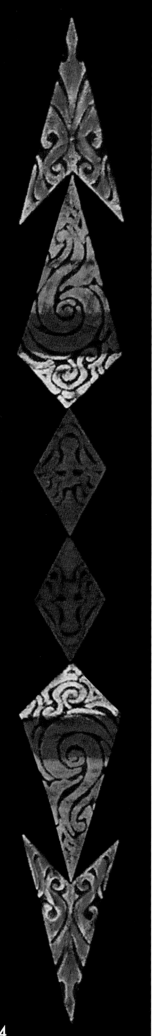

Welcome

My artistic aspirations are similar to the Star Trek mission: Going where no one has gone before," and I also want to get there at warp speed. Complexity and speed are not always easy partners. As a quilt maker, I am drawn to complex circular images, such as those comprising Paula Nadelstern's magnificent kaleidoscope quilts, but I lack the time and patience for labor intensive drafting and precision piecing techniques. I love surface design of all kinds and in my experiences with fabric paints, dyes, and foils, etc., my goal has been to always find and use the most direct and quickest path to my desired result.

As I experimented and designed, I found Shiva® Artist's Paintstiks® perfectly suit my "need for speed." Then my aspirations, passion, and experience came together and the StarBuilder concept was born. Now I, and others like me, can experience a partnership of both desires.

> *Using numerous color combinations, I could quickly create exactly what I wanted via easy Paintstik rubbings.*

I frequently ask "what if?" when I am designing. One day, while using a rectangular rubber stamp as texture for rubbing, I asked: "What if the stamps came in various shapes that fit together in a circle? Further, "what if I used the shapes as textures for rubbings and then used those shapes with fusible appliqué techniques to create designs?" The envisioned process would leapfrog right over drafting, fussy cutting, and piecing challenges—a thrilling concept!

To test the idea, I drafted a Mariner's Compass star design, as it provided the necessary shapes.

Then I etched designs inspired by Maori tattoo designs on the shapes and sent my ideas off to be created. (If you are wondering why Maori tattoo designs, it's not that I sport body tattoos, I simply have an eclectic set of art interests).

The prototype stamps arrived and surpassed my expectations. Using numerous color combinations, I could quickly create exactly what I wanted via easy Paintstik rubbings. Fusibles provided freedom from piecing restrictions. I could build up layers of shapes, space the shapes apart, or overlap them without limitation. Best of all, I achieved dramatic results in a matter of hours instead of in weeks or months.

My husband painted while I applied fusibles to the back of the shapes, cut them out, then arranged them into dazzling designs. For me, the design process requires physically moving shapes around. Designs do not just pop into my head; they are built one shape at a time. I never know what the end result will be and I find that exploration process exciting.

I've loved every minute of creativity the StarBuilders have given me. This book is intended to offer you basic skills and inspire you to launch your own unique explorations.

The possibilities are infinite—thank you for sharing my adventure,

-Laura

Perseus Star

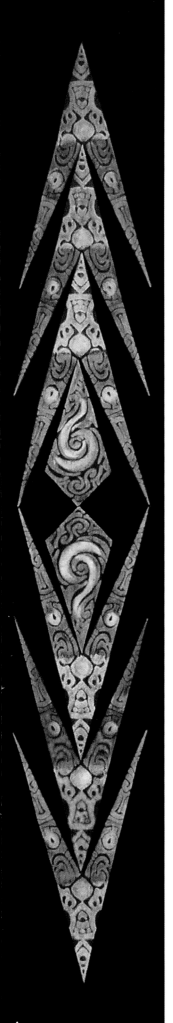

Overview

What is a StarBuilder, anyway?

A StarBuilder is an unmounted 6" x 9" rubber stamp containing various shapes. I gave each shape a "pet" name.

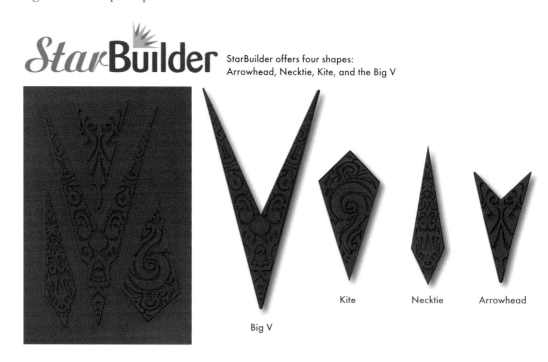

StarBuilder offers four shapes: Arrowhead, Necktie, Kite, and the Big V

Big V

Kite

Necktie

Arrowhead

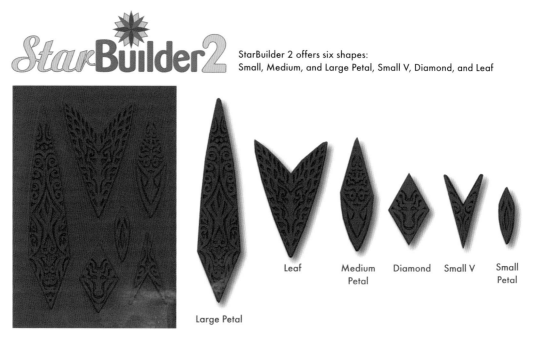

StarBuilder 2 offers six shapes: Small, Medium, and Large Petal, Small V, Diamond, and Leaf

Large Petal

Leaf

Medium Petal

Diamond

Small V

Small Petal

You can use these shapes to create an infinite variety of stars by arranging them in a circle that radiates from a center point. In addition to stars, the shapes can be arranged to make other images, such as birds, fish, flowers, design motifs, or borders.

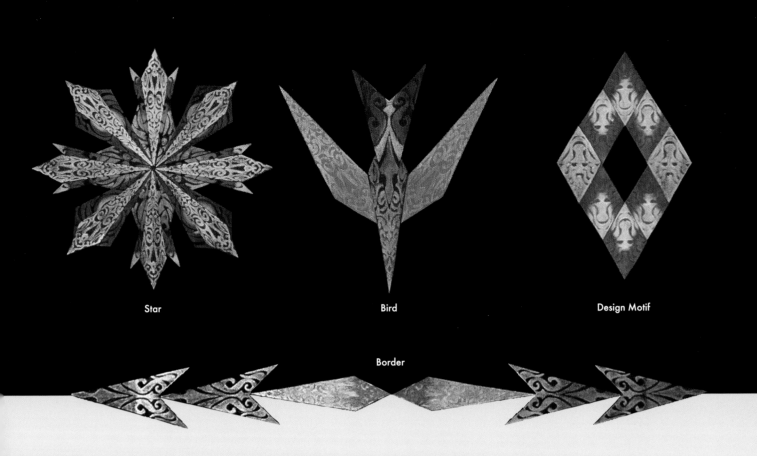

Star

Bird

Design Motif

Border

How the StarBuilder process works: a summary

No seam allowances and no sewing are required to construct the designs shown in *StarBuilder Inspirations*. The unique shapes of the StarBuilders are the basis for Paintstik rubbings which produce unique fabric pieces. Fusible appliqué techniques then provide quick and easy arrangement and placement, and the process ends with the final fusing.

1 Paint the shapes

2 Apply fusible

3 Cut shapes out

4 Arrange the shapes

5 Fuse

Gathering the Necessities

In addition to the StarBuilder, you'll need the following supplies

Shiva Artist iridescent Paintstiks

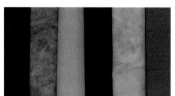

The more colors, the better! I strongly prefer iridescent Paintstiks, because they make my designs "glow" and show fabulously on dark fabrics. *Note:* Shiva Artist Paintstiks are also available in a matte finish, which I seldom use for rubbings as the colors tend to flow more thickly than iridescents, which makes it difficult to achieve a crisp image on finer detailed shapes. There are two matte colors used in this book though, matte napthol red and azo orange, as those specific colors are not available in an iridescent form.

Fabric

I prefer cottons, but you can use silks and synthetics. Do avoid fabrics that ravel excessively.

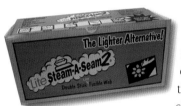

Double-sided fusible web

The fusibles are sold by yard (usually near the cutting table) at fabric stores, or in packages found in the notions department. I generally use *Lite Steam-A-Seam 2*. *Steam-A-Seam 2* is a heavier web. Both have a unique pressure-sensitive coating on both sides that allows for a temporary hold until permanently fused with an iron. Without the temporary hold, it would be necessary to pin the shapes to hold them in place—very time consuming. *Note:* Steam-A-Seam without the "2" at the end of the name does *not* have the pressure-sensitive coating, making it similar to regular fusible.

Parchment paper

You'll find this on the grocery store shelf near wax paper and aluminum foil.

No-slip mat

I use the Grip-n-Grip mat by Bear Thread Designs. It prevents slippage by holding the fabric and stamps exactly where you put them.

360° Protractor, transparency film, permanent sharpie markers

These supplies, used for making orientation templates, are available in office supply stores.

General workroom supplies

Other necessities include a steam iron, ironing board, erasable marking pencils or chalk, paper toweling, cutting mat, rotary cutter, ruler, scissors, plastic or newspaper for covering work surface, and disposable wipes for removing paint from hands.

Delta Star

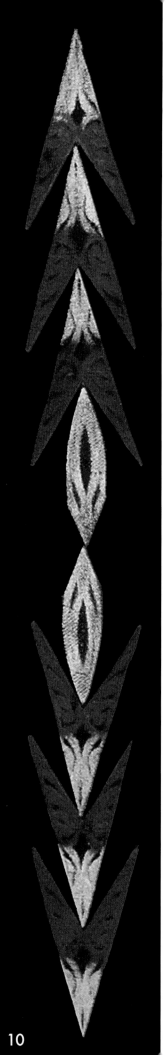

Getting Ready

Cut the stamps apart

Cut the stamps apart leaving approximately a quarter inch edge around each shape. Mounting the stamps is NOT necessary when using them with paintstiks.

Select fabrics

Fabric color makes a difference! It becomes an important part of the overall design as the paint won't cover the grooves in the stamp. Wherever the grooves are, the original fabric color remains exposed.

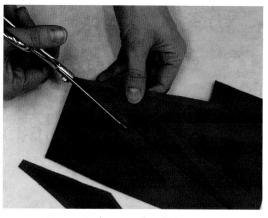

Leave ¼" edge around each shape

Choose darks and brights in solid colors, or subtle tone-on-tone fabrics. I prefer very dark, black, or bright colors in solids, or a subtle tone-on-tone which reads like a solid. The objective is for the background color to show evenly on each shape, which means avoiding plaid, floral, or any fabric with significant color or texture variations.

Dark charcoal
background fabric

Red/orange
background fabric

Suitable Deep Darks

  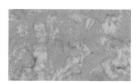 

Suitable Brights

Prepare Fabrics

Prewash your fabric to remove any sizing, etc. Use regular laundry detergent without bleach or softener additives. Do not use softener or dryer sheets. Press the fabric to remove any wrinkles

Prepare Work Surface

Wear old clothes or a smock and cover your work surface with plastic or newspapers. Small pieces of paint will get on your work surface, your clothes, and your hands. The paint easily comes off skin with soap and water or wipes.

Choose Paintstiks

Contrasts in values offer the "wow" factor. The larger your on-hand selection, the more options you'll have for your painting palette. If you start with just a few colors, be sure to select at least one each from the light, medium, and dark value groups. The colors used throughout this book are shown below.

Iridescent light
gold, orange, pink

Medium value: iridescent copper, green, gold, , leaf green,
purple, turquoise; matt azo orange, napthol red

Dark value: iridescent blue,
charcoal, brown, red

Prepare Paintstiks

Paintstiks have a protective skin on the outer surface, which must be removed before the paint can flow. The skin begins to heal soon after you stop painting. The skin prevents the paint from drying out, whether you use them the following day, or years in the future.

To remove the skin, place the end of the Paintstik into about four layers of folded paper toweling, and twist into it. At first you'll feel friction, but as you rub, the skin will transfer to the toweling and feel slippery. A gentle touch is not effective— grip firmly and twist hard. I use my fingernail through the toweling if the paint seems stubborn. If you have difficulty with the paper towel method for removing the film, use a small paring knife and remove a very small layer from the surface of the paintstik. Then, use the toweling to smooth all skin from the end of the Paintstik.

Laura's Hints 'n' Tips
To remove unwanted "crumbs" from the fabric, take a piece of scotch tape or masking tape and press straight down and then lift straight up.

Always keep the end of the Paintstik clear of *all* skin. **This procedure must be repeated every few minutes** to prevent unwanted pieces of skin from getting on your work. As you work the skin away, strive to maintain the original rounded shape of the Paintstik end. As the Paintstik wears down, loosen the cardboard wrapping and push the end up from the bottom.

Remove Paintstik skin

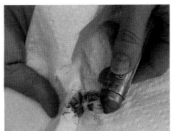

Frequently remove Paintstik skin
as you work

Maintain rounded tip

Rubbings

Assumptions

The old adage about assumptions was never more true! I've watched hundreds of people take their first Paintstik for a test drive and I can say with great certainty that past knowledge about crayons, coloring, and stamping, greatly interferes with learning the rubbing technique. The *next pages are critical to your success*, so please *read carefully*. Not to worry though, everything you need to know to produce spectacular results is coming right up!

With just a little practice, you'll soon feel very good about your Paintstik rubbing technique.

Get a grip!

Some people write by holding a pencil loosely near the eraser end—but holding a Paintstik that way is not a good thing, because you won't be able to exert sufficient pressure with a loose grip. Also, the Paintstik will annoyingly slide up the protective cardboard wrapping if you are not holding it firmly. Hold the wrapper firmly with about ¾" of the Paintstik end exposed.

Hold wrapper firmly with about ¾" of the Paintstik end exposed

Paint the fabric

Never paint directly on the stamp. If you have used liquid fabric paint with stamps it seems reasonable to first paint the rubber stamp and then print on the fabric. BAD ASSUMPTION. The Paintstik won't print well, and think about it, even if it did work, why would you want to use two steps, when you want paint on the fabric in the first place?

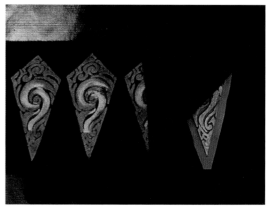

Always place fabric on TOP of the stamp

Laura's Hints 'n' Tips

I am right handed, so I start painting on the far left of the fabric strip.

That way, my hand never touches the painted fabric

(which may cause smudging).

Lefties, do the opposite.

Crayons: fuhgetaboutit!

We all have muscle memory from our past experience with crayons, causing us to press down, and rub back and forth in both directions. ANOTHER BAD ASSUMPTION. This will cause the fabric to slip and you'll end up with blurry images.

Do your rubbings in one direction only, away from your body, using short strokes about 1" long. Use your non-painting hand as an anchor to hold the fabric firmly and prevent slippage.

You must apply pressure evenly to cover the fabric with enough paint for the image to clearly show, but not so much that you have a thick buildup of paint which will take a long time to dry and may flake off. Experiment with pressure until you get the desired amount of color on the fabric.

 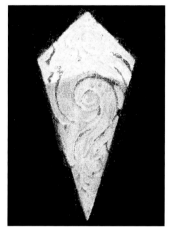 

Too little   Too much   Just Right

The amount of pressure required for smooth flowing varies by color. This is owing to the pigments and is perfectly normal for Paintstiks. Successful rubbings require a variety of motions all happening at once. With just a little practice this will soon happen automatically.

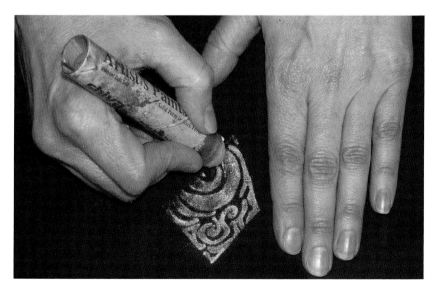

Hold Paintstik firmly. Use your non-painting hand as an "anchor" near the edge of stamp. Use short strokes, beginning at the edge of the stamp to rub in one direction AWAY from body.

Do's	Don'ts
essential	**ineffective**
Rub in one direction only, away from your anchor hand.	Rub back and forth, in both directions. That causes the fabric to bunch and means blurry designs.
Avoid touching the fresh paint.	Rub into the paint with your hands. This will smear the design and remove color from the image.
Experiment with pressure to find the best coverage. Find the "sweet spot," and paint the image evenly.	Rub too lightly or the color won't be intense; rub too heavily or the paint may build up excessively.
Use your non-painting hand as an anchor to prevent slippage.	Shift the fabric while painting, which will cause blurry designs.
Paint the entire image, all the way from tip to tip, covering the entire image.	Fail to get paint all the way to the tips and outer edges. This will cause the loss of cutting lines and an uneven appearance between duplicate shapes.

Laura's Hints 'n' Tips

Using a Grip-n-Grip no-slip mat under your StarBuilder stamp will help keep both the fabric and the stamp from moving. If you are having a lot of trouble with fabric slipping across the stamp surface, spray the stamp with a temporary spray adhesive.

Grip-n-Grip prevents slippage

Libra Star

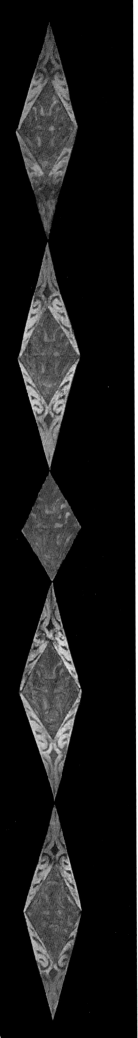

Color Strategy

Dramatic results

Paint your fabric with one color or several. The actual color is much less important than the value contrast. You achieve the most dramatic effects with strong value contrast (light to dark) of adjacent colors. My approach is to stand back several feet from a test swatch and squint (or take off my glasses). If I don't see sufficient contrast, I choose a more suitable color.

Value and contrast make a big difference

In the three value images, notice the difference in appearance when the same colors (iridescent gold, turquoise, and red) are applied to light, medium and dark background fabrics.

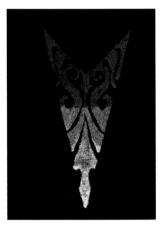

| Light value background | Medium value background | Dark value background |

Color placement

Basic coloring variations when using the StarBuilder shapes include:

Single color: Just one color used.

Parfait color: Paint appears in stripes of color across the surface of the fabric. Depending on the size of the stamp, additional stripes of color can be added to the fabric. The more stripes, the more complex and interesting the final design will become.

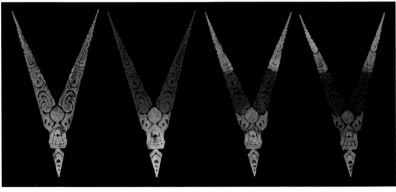

One color

2 color, 3 color, 4 color, 5 color progression

Laura's Hints 'n' Tips
When using multiple colors, always "touch up"
before moving the fabric to ensure smooth color transition.

Layering color: Paintstiks allow layering of one color on top of another. This is done before removing the fabric from the stamp shape. There's no need for the paint to dry before adding another color.

Step 1: iridescent purple   Step 2: iridescent gold added

Partitioned color: Uses colors to feature specific design areas.

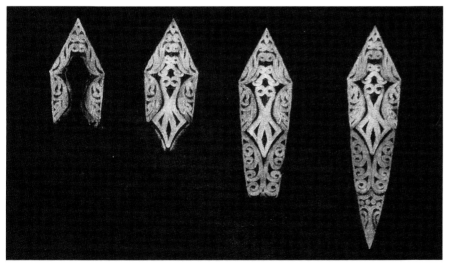

Multiple colors partitioning sequence

Duplicating Images

Achieving the kaleidoscope effect requires duplicates of each shape, with the objective to make them as similar as possible. There will be tiny variations—just like in nature—for the work of the hand never does exact duplicates.

As you paint the duplicates, it is very important to always refer to the original design. If you look at the last one you painted, instead of the original, and repeat that 24 times, you may find your results resemble the consequences of a children's game of Round Robin.

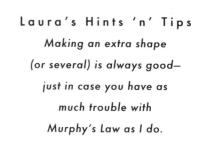

Storing Shapes

Store your shapes by using a large paper clip or wire clothes pin to hold them together. As my collection of painted shapes expanded, I organized them in small plastic containers labeled with the shape name. The larger your collection, the more fun it is to play with possibilities!

Store shapes

Troubleshooting Tips

Problem	Solution
Paint is not flowing smoothly.	Be sure the skin is completely removed from the end of the Paintstik. Try different areas of the stick to find the "sweet spot."
Chunks of skin are appearing on the fabric.	Remove skin with the sticky side of masking tape or scotch tape, etc. Make sure that you press the tape straight down, then lift straight up, do not rub back and forth. If skin often appears on the fabric, it means the Paintstik needs to be wiped more frequently to keep the end smooth and free from skin.
Smudging outside the lines.	No problem, the shapes are cut on the lines and those smudges will get thrown out with the scrap fabric.
Fabric shifts, causing smudging of the design.	Firmly hold fabric down on the stamp with your anchor hand. I always use a no-slip mat (called a Grip-n-Grip) which helps keep both fabric and stamp in place. Note: even when done correctly, rubbings produce an unavoidable amount of slight smudging between the design lines. This is more noticeable on light colored fabric.
Paint seems too heavy or too light against the fabric.	Colors vary in the amount of pressure required to produce a nice flow. Always practice on scrap fabric until you are getting the desired effect.

How many shapes to make?

You can get a precise answer only if you know in advance what the end result will be. When you create one of the stars in this book, the count information is provided. Personally, I just keep on painting until I get to the end of the fabric strip, always happy to have a variety of shapes on hand and ready for experimentation.

Organize shapes to minimize waste

My frugal nature causes me to view every inch of fabric as precious (with no regard to the hundreds of yards of fabric that I already own). Achieve minimal waste by doing the rubbings on manageable widths of fabric, using the long edge as a guide, and moving the fabric as you work. Take care to not touch the already painted shapes, which causes smudging and paint removal. Allow approximately ¾" between each shape. Shown are some examples of various shapes painted in strips.

Cut fabric into manageable widths

5" width   6" width   11" width

Don't sweat the small stuff

Close inspection of my stars will reveal some tiny imperfections, slight variations of coloration, and spacing. Clue: do you see anything amiss with the Orion star on page 21?

Only machines can be consistently exact. Humans are part of nature and nature never does anything exactly the same way twice. Each of us gets to choose our standards and I chose not to discard the Orion Star. It's a lovely star, and serves as a reminder of the importance of double-checking placement before final fusing. Learn from each project, and cherish the work of your hands.

Orion Star

Fabric Care

After heat setting, your fabric is washable by hand or machine in cold water. Avoid pouring detergent directly on the painted areas of your fabric, and use a low setting on your dryer or line dry.

Don't dry clean

Never dry clean fabric embellished with Paintstik color. Dry cleaning fluid is a solvent that may remove the paint from your fabric. If that happens, you'd lose all your creative endeavors.

Drying time & heat setting

Paintstik color generally dries to the touch in 24 hours, but it usually takes several days for the paint to dry thoroughly when applied as a rubbing. After it dries, heat setting is required for fabric which will be washed. There is no need to heat set fabric used in projects that WILL NOT require laundering, but the paint may not be completely dry for several weeks. Heat setting can be done with an iron or home clothes dryer.

To heat set in a clothes dryer: After (and only after) the Paintstik color has dried for 3-5 days, place the fabric in a hot clothes dryer for 30 minutes.

To heat set with an iron: Place the project face down on parchment paper, or butcher Kraft paper; not directly on your ironing board cover. Set a dry iron to a temperature appropriate for the fabric and press each section of the fabric for 10-15 seconds. (Press, don't iron)

To heat set in a hurry: You can heat set **iridescent** Paintstik color without waiting for the paint to cure thoroughly, but there is a risk of removing small amounts of paint, and some colors may change in appearance. Be sure to try a small sample first. Take precautions by heat setting in a well ventilated area, and make sure you protect your ironing surface from oil stains.

Caution! Do not heat set matt colors in a hurry. Matt colors require 3 days of drying time before heat setting. The pigments interact with heat and are easily scorched.

Clean up

Wash your hands with soap and water to remove Paintstik color, or use disposable wipes. I sometimes wear surgical gloves, just to avoid getting paint under my fingernails. Cedar Canyon Textiles Brush Soap is great for cleaning hands, even under your fingernails, without drying your skin.

Star Building

Apply fusible web

To apply fusible web to the back of the painted fabric strips, remove the liner paper from one side of the Lite Steam-A-Seam 2. Discard the paper (tiny pieces of adhesive will stick to the paper, you don't want them on your iron or fabric).

Place the WRONG side of the painted fabric strip on the STICKY SIDE of the web. Position parchment paper over the top of the fabric to prevent exposed areas of the web from sticking to iron. Press with an iron until fused.

A thin film of web, covered by the second release paper, will be on the wrong side of the fabric.

Place wrong side of fabric on the web;
parchment paper on top and fuse

Cut along the outside edges of the shape

Cut out the shapes

Carefully cut out the painted shapes following their outside edges. Do not remove the second liner paper from the back of the shape until you are ready to assemble a star as it will cause the web to dry out.

If you have removed the paper, and change your mind about using the shape, not to worry. Save it for another star – the web can still be permanently fused effectively. (Once the paper is removed, the web gradually loses its pressure sensitive ability that gives the ability to temporarily stick to the background material. Temporary "sticking" is the feature that differentiates Steam-a-Seam2 from regular fusibles. However, the web will fuse when heat is applied, even after the pressure sensitive feature has been eliminated owing to prolonged exposure to air).

Select and Prepare Background Fabric

There are two approaches to choosing background fabric, which you choose depends on the answer to the question: Do I want to experiment with possibilities or do I know exactly what I am going to make?

The stars in this book resulted from my experimentation. I wanted to see what would happen with various combinations of shapes, with no particular thought on how the design would be used. I started with a base of solid black fabric cut into squares between 14 to 36 inches a side. I moved StarBuilder pieces around until I was happy with the results, and then I fused them to the black fabric. Most of the completed stars were later "liberated" by applying a fusible to the reverse of the black background fabric, cutting out the entire star, around the outer edge and then fusing it to a different fabric. This approach means your base fabric will never again see the light of day, so use fabric which you no longer care about (not the expensive hand dyed fabrics).

If you have made a final decision on your background fabric, select Paintstik colors which ensure sufficient value contrast.

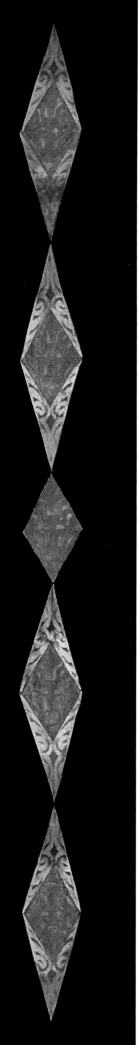

Mark orientation lines—unless you want crooked stars!

No one wants crooked stars. Orientation marks are necessary to ensure an even distance between the star points. It's almost as easy as 1, 2, 3: One is cutting a square, two is marking the center, and three is creating orientation lines.

Cut a Square: Construction of all the stars in this book begins in the center of a square. How large the square should be is driven by the desired diameter of the star. If you have a specific project in mind, you need to decide the size.

For example, a star with a diameter of 12" used to make an 18" pillow would need to be cut from an 18" square, PLUS seam allowance.

Mark the center: Fold the square in half, and then into fourths to locate the center point. Or measure with a ruler. Mark the center point with chalk or a marking pencil that can be easily removed. Draw a horizontal line through the center axis, dividing the fabric in half.

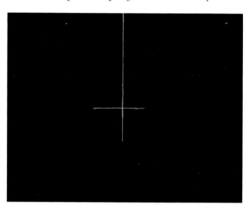

Mark the center

Create orientation templates

Stars are constructed in a circle, which has been divided into evenly spaced sections by lines radiating from the center axis point. Each line locates a "point" on a star. Stars may have 4, 5, 6, 7, 8, 10, 12, 16, 24 points, or more. Some of my early stars have points spaced unevenly because I wrongly thought I could position them "by the eye." It's easy to create orientation templates by using a 360° protractor, transparency sheets or clear stencil plastic and permanent markers.

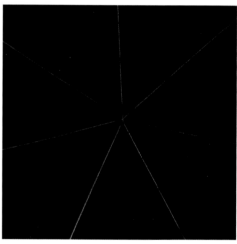

Orientation lines showing for 7-pointed star

Here's how made easy

Place a 360° protractor on a transparency. Use a marker to draw around the entire perimeter of the protractor and mark the center. *Do not move the protractor until all the marking is finished.*

The number of lines needed is found by dividing the desired number of points into 360°. Use a protractor to mark each point on the transparency within the drawn circle.

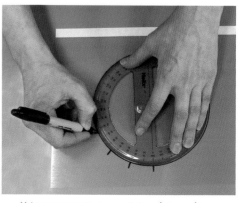

Using a protractor to create template markings

Multi-purpose templates without confusion

I've given you the segmenting "recipes" for stars with seven different point possibilities. There are three templates, two with two point recipes, one with three point possibilities. To keep from being confused as you work, the tables are color coded. Use two different color markers (three for the appropriate template) when you create your templates.

For 5- or 10-point star templates, divide 360° by 10 points to get 36°. Mark the template at:

0°	36°	72°	108°	144°	180°	216°	252°	288°	324°

For 8- or 16-point star templates, divide 360° by 16 points to get 22.5°. Mark the template at:

0°	22.5°	45°	67.5°	90°	112.5°	135°	157.5°
180°	202.5°	225°	247.5°	270°	292.5°	315°	337.5°

For 6-, 12-, or 24-point star templates, divide 360° by 24 points to get 15°. Mark the template at:

0°	15°	30°	45°	60°	75°	90°	105°	120°	135°	150°	165°
180°	195°	210°	225°	240°	255°	270°	285°	300°	315°	330°	345°

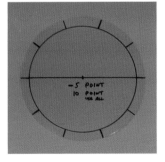

5- or 10-point template

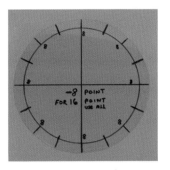

8- or 16-point template

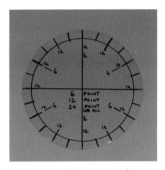

6-, 12-, or 24-point template

Cut around the template. Line up the center of the template with the center of your fabric square. Mark the orientation points on the fabric. Remove the template and connect all the lines through the center point.

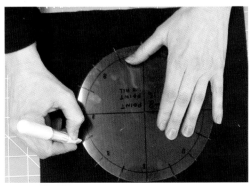

Center the template, and mark orientation points

Use ruler to connect and extend the lines

Layout strategies

The StarBuilder painted shapes, used individually or in combinations, can create dramatic variations.

To begin, peel off remaining paper liner (leaving the web of the fabric).

For stars, start with the center point and place the center of the shape directly over the orientation line.

Remove paper liner

Same shape – many points
(medium petal shape used in example)

5-point	6-point	7-point	12-point

Shapes can be layered, one on top of the other.

Step 1: 4 kites	Step 2: 4 contrasting kites	Step 3: 4 neckties

Flip around for different effects

Step 1: 4 kites	Step 2: 4 contrasting kites	Step 3: 8 neckties

Fitting the edges in various ways

6 diamond edges fitted together

diamonds spaced apart

8 leaves overlapped

Cut apart to form new shapes

Step 1: Cut 8 medium petals apart

Step 2: One section used
in 8-point star

Step 3: Second section used
in whirligig design

Placed in a straight line for border effects

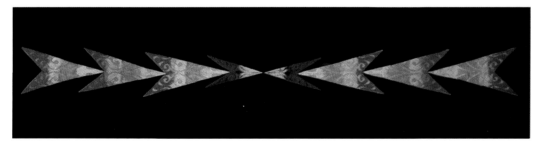

This isn't the end, only the beginning of possibilities!

Laura's Hints 'n' Tips

When choosing colors for shapes, I paint single shapes

in several variations to see what works best before making duplicates.

Fabric Fusing & Finishing

Be Happy

I find it best to avoid the final fusing until I am completely happy with the design and have double-checked the spacing. I love the "what if" game, and am very prone to changing color combinations during the assembly process

Fusing

Start in the center: Check continually to make sure the shapes have not moved before placing the iron on the shapes.

Press: (do *not* iron back and forth), for 10-15 seconds for cotton fabric (adjust temperature and fusing time to fabric) with a steam iron. Slightly overlap pressed areas until fusing is complete. Ironing back and forth may cause the shapes to shift.

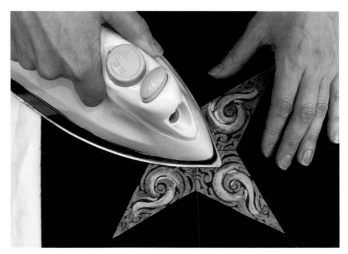

Fusing

Finishing

Remove the orientation marks. Sew around the edges of the fused shapes. I always do this using mono-filament thread and a small zigzag stitch. This ensures permanence over time, particularly for laundered projects.

Sigma Star

Laura's Hints 'n' Tips

Use the tip of the iron to "spot fuse" if shapes become unruly.

You should be able to remove them if you change

your mind about placement.

Gallery Introduction

The following galleries provide step-by-step instructions for dozens of dazzling designs.

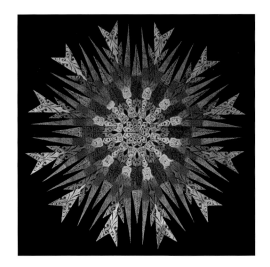

*Star*Builder
GALLERY
Pages 30-41

*Star*Builder2
GALLERY
Pages 42-53

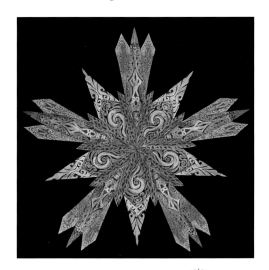

*Star*Builder *Star*Builder2
COMBO GALLERY
Pages 54-65

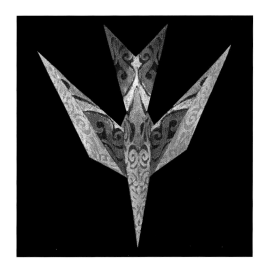

Shape Shifters
GALLERY
Pages 66-73

For further inspiration visit the Artist Gallery on pages 74-79.

Andromeda

This star requires 8 orientation points and uses five shapes. You will need:

4 kites (a)

4 kites (b)

4 arrowheads

8 neckties (a & c)

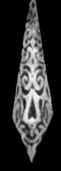

8 neckties (b)

Step

1

Shapes required:
4 kites (a)
Diameter: **9"**

Step

2

Shapes required
4 kites (b)
Diameter: **9"**

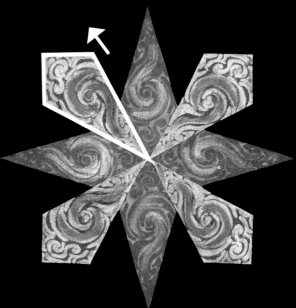

step

3

Shapes required:
4 arrowheads
4 neckties (a)

Diameter: **13"**

step

4

Shapes required:
8 neckties (b)
4 neckties (c)

Diameter: **14"**

Andromeda Colors:

Iridescent – **green, gold, leaf green, light gold, pink, purple, red, turquoise**

Aries

This star requires 12 orientation points and uses four shapes. You will need:

**6
kites**

**6
arrowheads (a)**

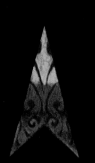

**6
arrowheads (b)**

**6
neckties**

Step 1

Shapes required:
6 kites

Diameter: **9"**

Step 2

Shapes required
6 arrowheads (a)

Diameter: **9"**

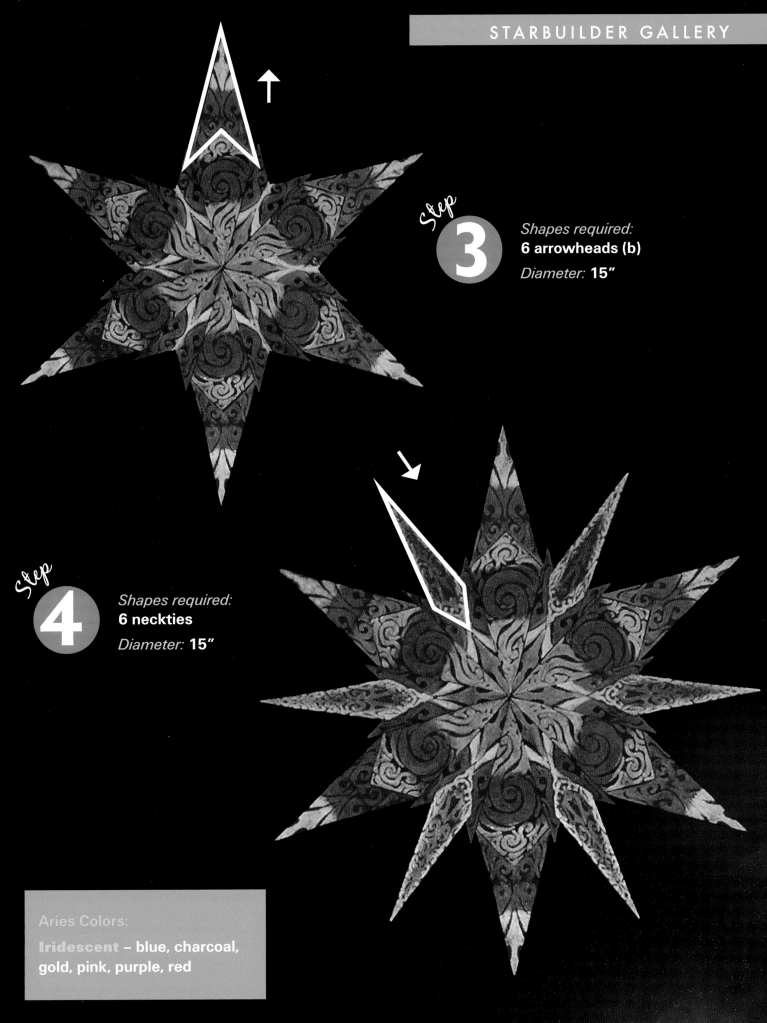

step

3

Shapes required:
6 arrowheads (b)

Diameter: **15"**

step

4

Shapes required:
6 neckties

Diameter: **15"**

Aries Colors:

Iridescent – blue, charcoal, gold, pink, purple, red

Crux

This star requires 8 orientation points and uses seven shapes. You will need:

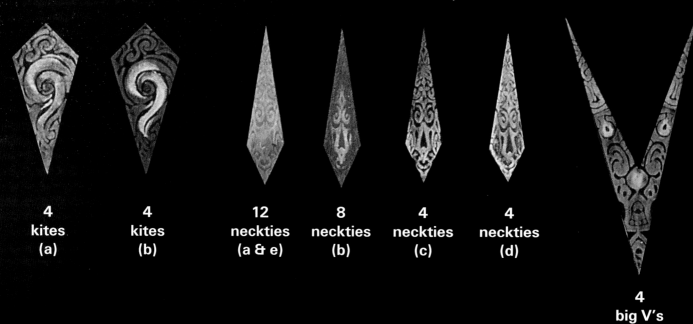

4 kites (a)   **4 kites (b)**   **12 neckties (a & e)**   **8 neckties (b)**   **4 neckties (c)**   **4 neckties (d)**

4 big V's

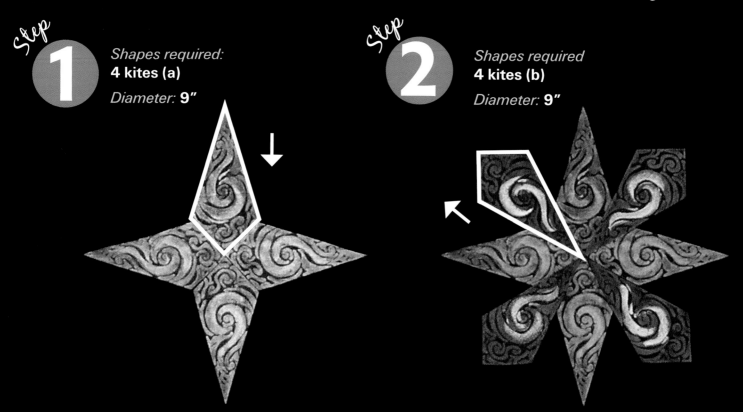

step 1

Shapes required:
4 kites (a)
Diameter: **9"**

step 2

Shapes required
4 kites (b)
Diameter: **9"**

Crux Colors:

Iridescent – blue, charcoal, gold, purple, red, turquoise

34

step

3

Shapes required:
8 neckties (a)

Diameter: **12"**

step

4

Shapes required:
8 neckties (b)
4 neckties (c)
4 neckties (d)
4 neckties (e)
4 big V's

Diameter: **18"**

Electra

This star requires 8 orientation points and uses two shapes. You will need:

8 arrowheads

12 neckties (a)

12 neckties (b)

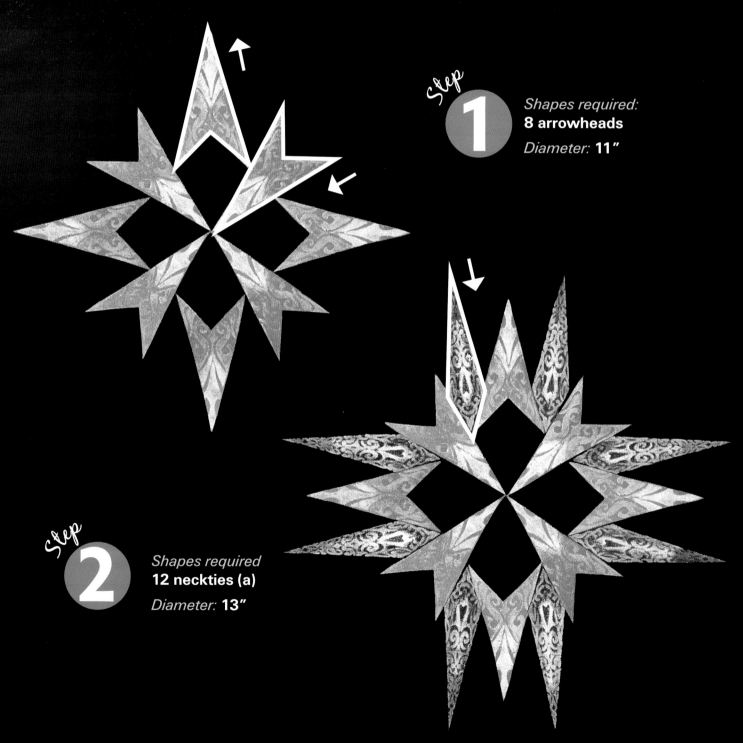

step 1

Shapes required:
8 arrowheads
Diameter: **11"**

step 2

Shapes required
12 neckties (a)
Diameter: **13"**

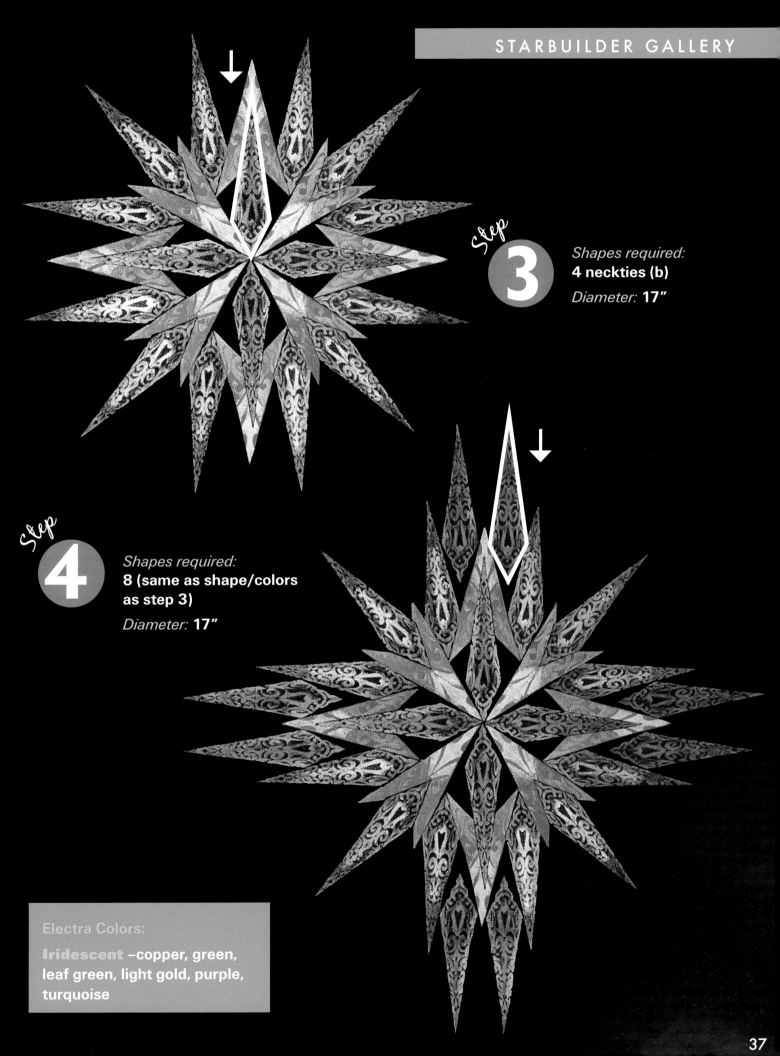

step

3

Shapes required:
4 neckties (b)
Diameter: **17"**

step

4

Shapes required:
8 (same as shape/colors as step 3)
Diameter: **17"**

Electra Colors:

Iridescent –copper, green, leaf green, light gold, purple, turquoise

Orion

This star requires 8 orientation points and uses five shapes. You will need:

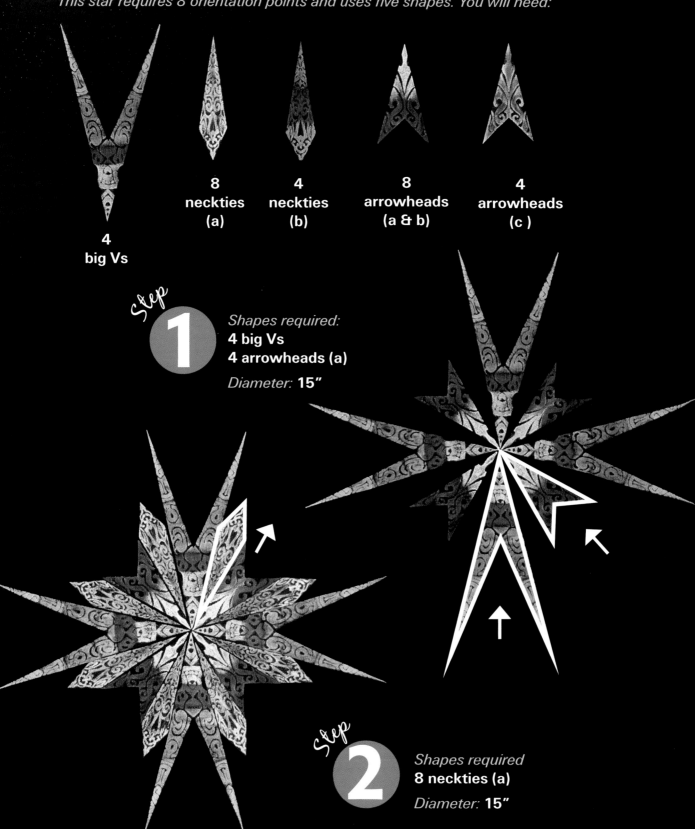

**4
big Vs**

**8
neckties
(a)**

**4
neckties
(b)**

**8
arrowheads
(a & b)**

**4
arrowheads
(c)**

step 1

Shapes required:
4 big Vs
4 arrowheads (a)
Diameter: **15"**

step 2

Shapes required
8 neckties (a)
Diameter: **15"**

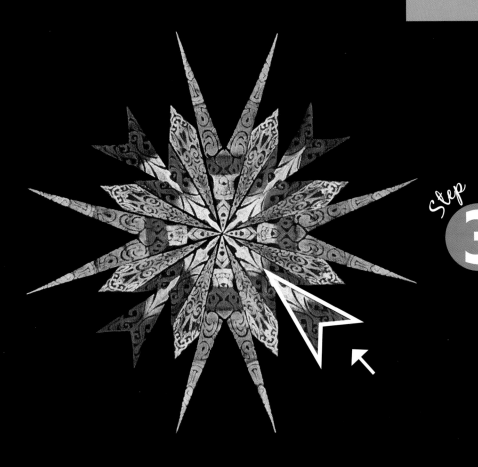

Step

3

Shapes required:
4 arrowheads (b)

Diameter: **15"**

Step

4

Shapes required:
4 arrowheads (c)
4 neckties (b)

Diameter: **17"**

Orion Colors:

Iridescent – **gold, leaf green, light gold, orange, red, turquoise**

Pisces

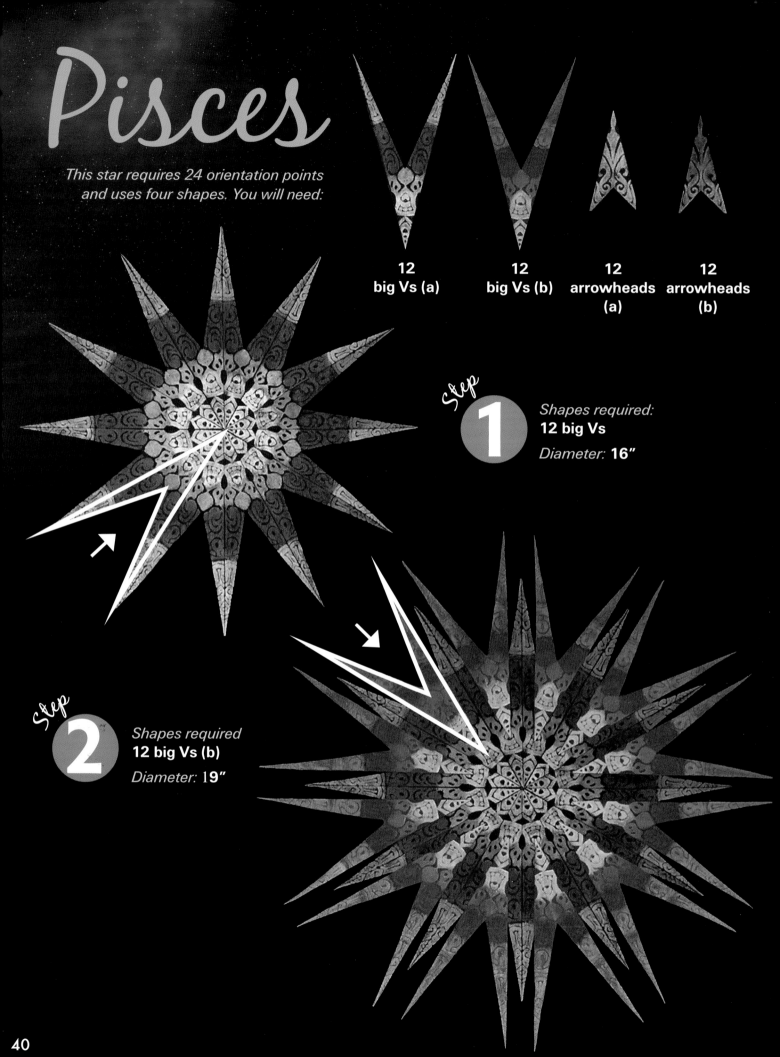

This star requires 24 orientation points and uses four shapes. You will need:

12 big Vs (a)

12 big Vs (b)

12 arrowheads (a)

12 arrowheads (b)

step 1

Shapes required:
12 big Vs
Diameter: **16"**

step 2

Shapes required
12 big Vs (b)
Diameter: **19"**

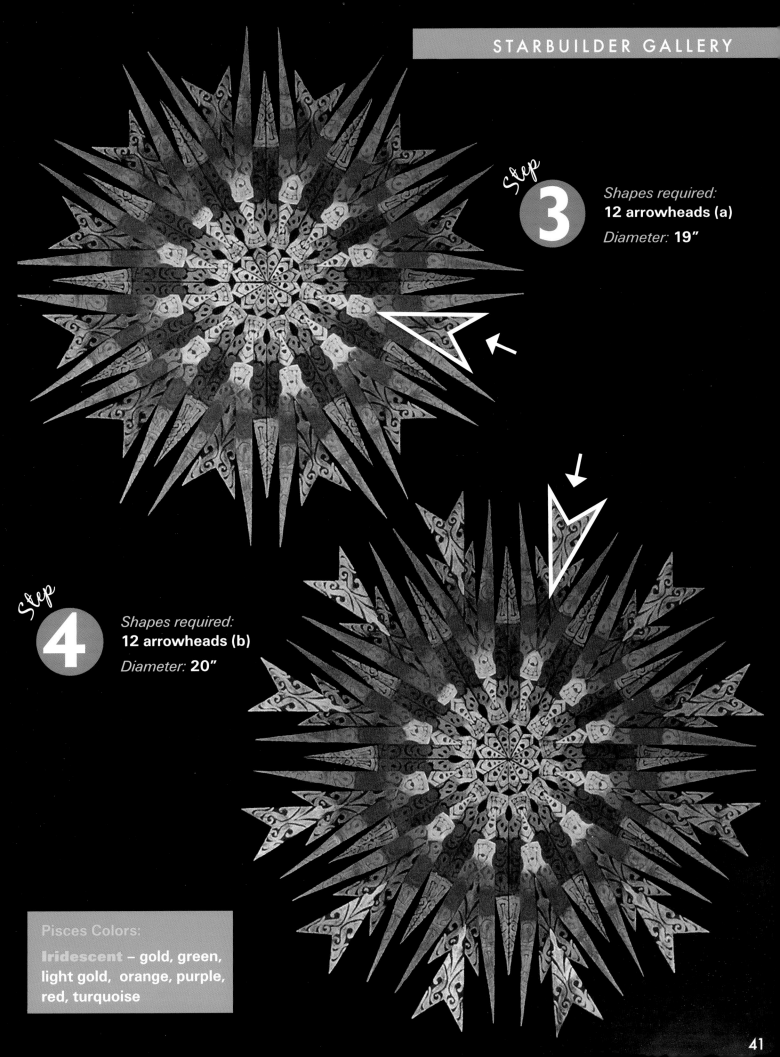

step
3

Shapes required:
12 arrowheads (a)
Diameter: **19"**

step
4

Shapes required:
12 arrowheads (b)
Diameter: **20"**

Pisces Colors:

Iridescent – **gold, green, light gold, orange, purple, red, turquoise**

41

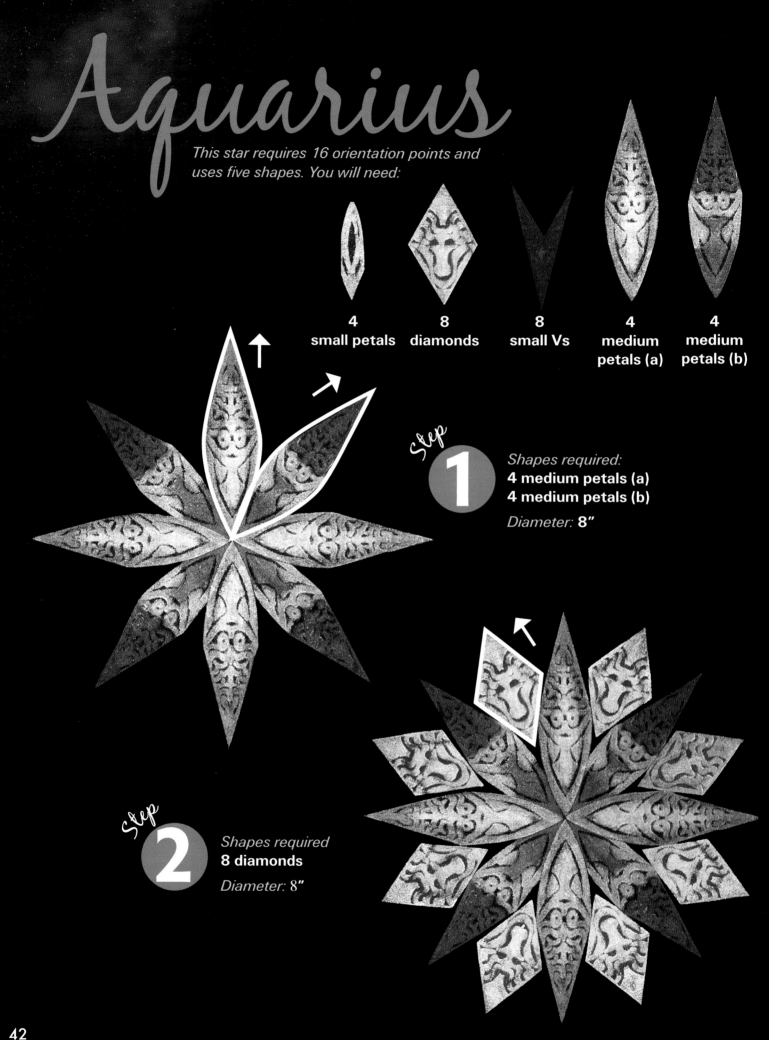

Aquarius

This star requires 16 orientation points and uses five shapes. You will need:

4 small petals

8 diamonds

8 small Vs

4 medium petals (a)

4 medium petals (b)

step **1**

Shapes required:
4 medium petals (a)
4 medium petals (b)

Diameter: **8"**

step **2**

Shapes required
8 diamonds

Diameter: 8"

Step
3

Shapes required:
8 small Vs

Diameter: **10"**

Step
4

Shapes required:
4 small petals

Diameter: **10"**

Aquarius Colors:

Iridescent – gold, light gold, pink, purple, turquoise

Matt – napthol red

Carina

This star requires 24 orientation points and uses four shapes. You will need:

12 diamonds

12 small Vs (a)

12 small Vs (b)

12 small Vs (c)

step 1

Shapes required:
12 small Vs (a)
Diameter: **5″**

step 2

Shapes required
12 diamonds
Diameter: **8″**

44

step
3

Shapes required:
12 small Vs (b)

Diameter: **11"**

step
4

Shapes required:
12 small Vs (c)

Diameter: **11"**

Carina Colors:

Iridescent – **brown, copper, gold, turquoise**

Corona Borealis

This star requires 8 orientation points and uses four shapes. You will need:

8
medium petals

8
leaves (a)

8
leaves (b)

4
small petals

step
1

Shapes required:
8 medium petals
Diameter: **8"**

step
2

Shapes required
8 leaves (a)
Diameter: **10"**

step
3

Shapes required:
8 leaves (b)
Diameter: **14"**

step
4

Shapes required:
4 small petals
Diameter: **14"**

Corona Borealis Colors:

Iridescent – **copper, gold, leaf green, light gold, purple, red**

Matt – **napthol red**

47

Pegasus

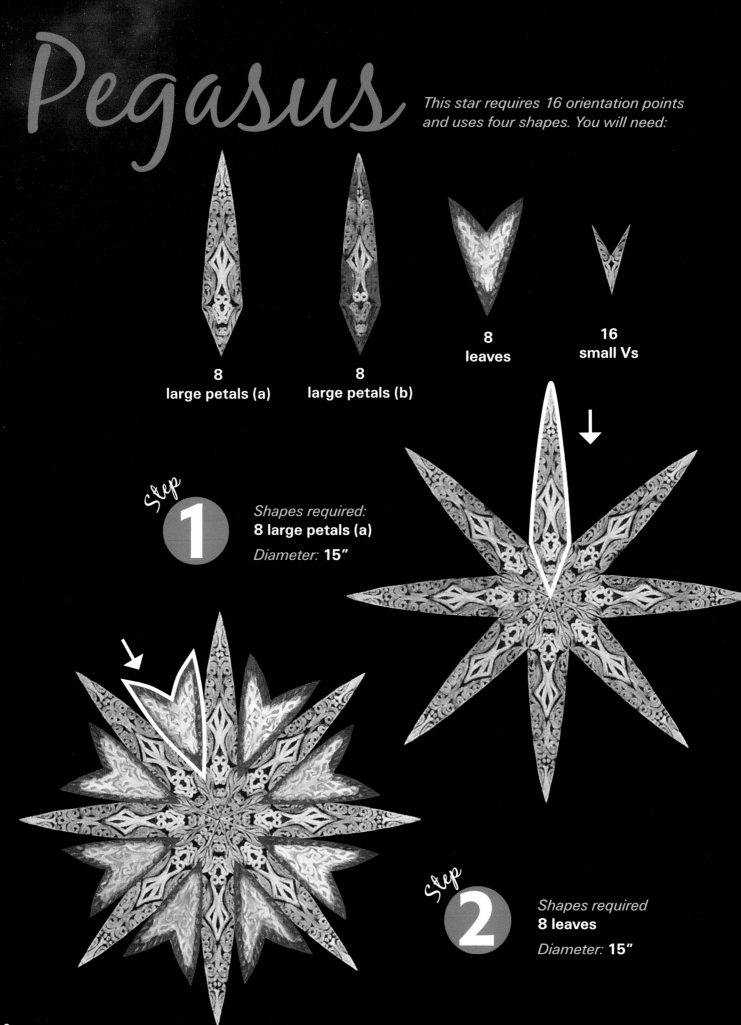

8
large petals (a)

8
large petals (b)

8
leaves

16
small Vs

step

1

Shapes required:
8 large petals (a)
Diameter: **15″**

step

2

Shapes required
8 leaves
Diameter: **15″**

48

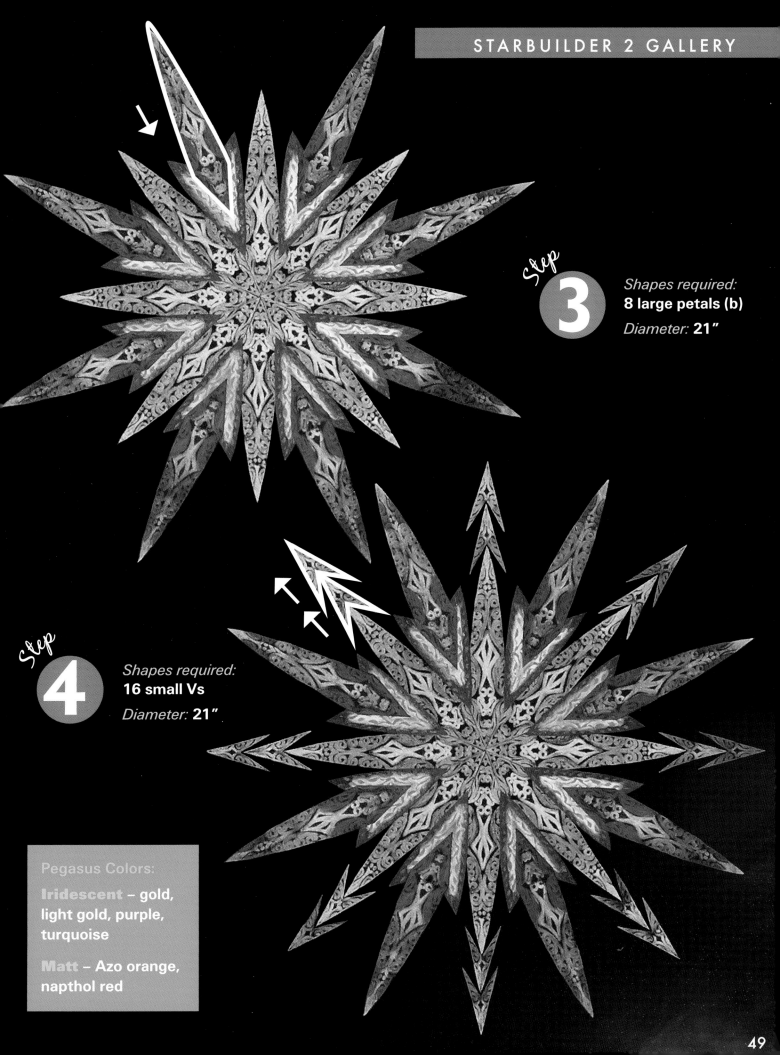

Step

3

Shapes required:
8 large petals (b)

Diameter: **21"**

Step

4

Shapes required:
16 small Vs

Diameter: **21"**

Pegasus Colors:

Iridescent – **gold, light gold, purple, turquoise**

Matt – **Azo orange, napthol red**

49

Tucana

This star requires 24 orientation points and uses seven shapes. You will need:

6 leaves	**6** medium petals (a)	**6** medium petals (b)	**6** medium petals (c)	**12** medium petals (d)	**6** small petals

6 large petals

step 1

Shapes required:
6 leaves
Diameter: **15"**

step 2

Shapes required
6 large petals
Diameter: **15"**

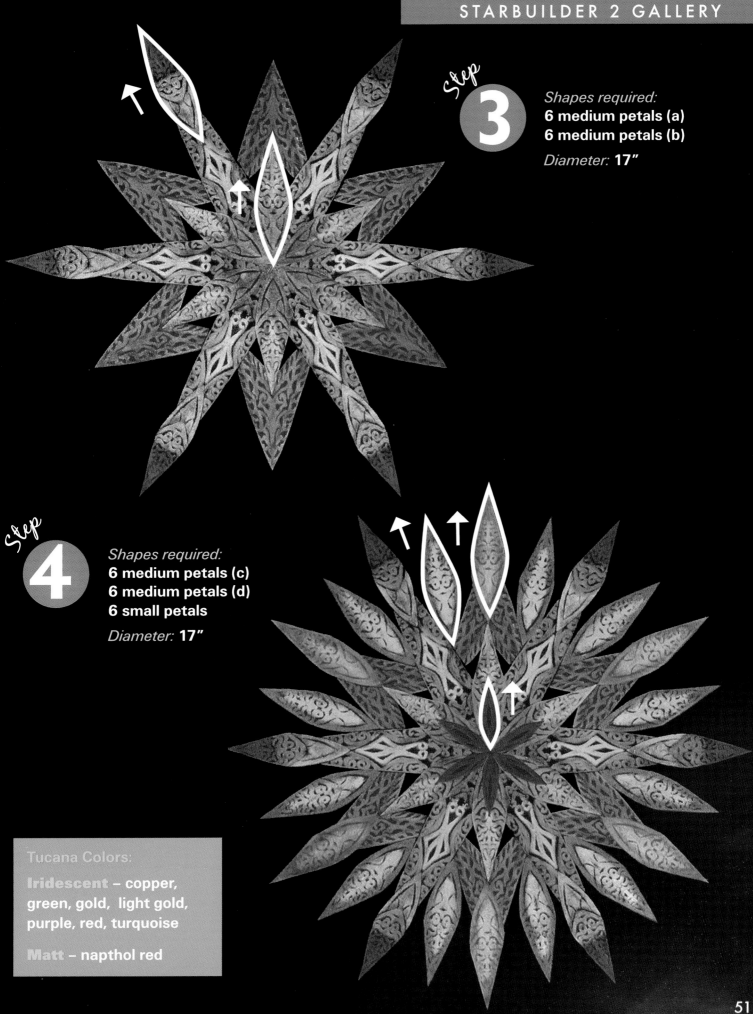

step

3

Shapes required:
6 medium petals (a)
6 medium petals (b)

Diameter: **17"**

step

4

Shapes required:
6 medium petals (c)
6 medium petals (d)
6 small petals

Diameter: **17"**

Tucana Colors:

Iridescent – copper, green, gold, light gold, purple, red, turquoise

Matt – napthol red

51

Ursa Minor

This star requires 32 orientation points and uses five shapes. You will need:

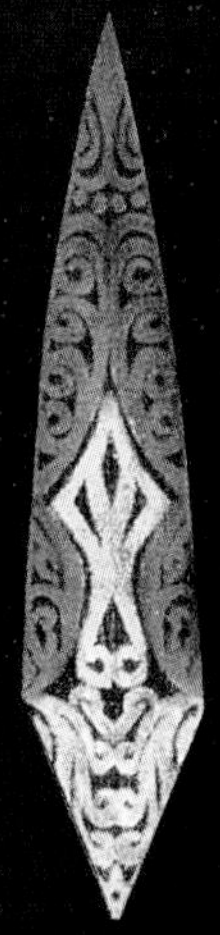

16 diamonds

8 small Vs

16 small petals

8 large petals (a)

8 large petals (b)

step 1

Shapes required:
8 large petals (a)

Diameter: **15"**

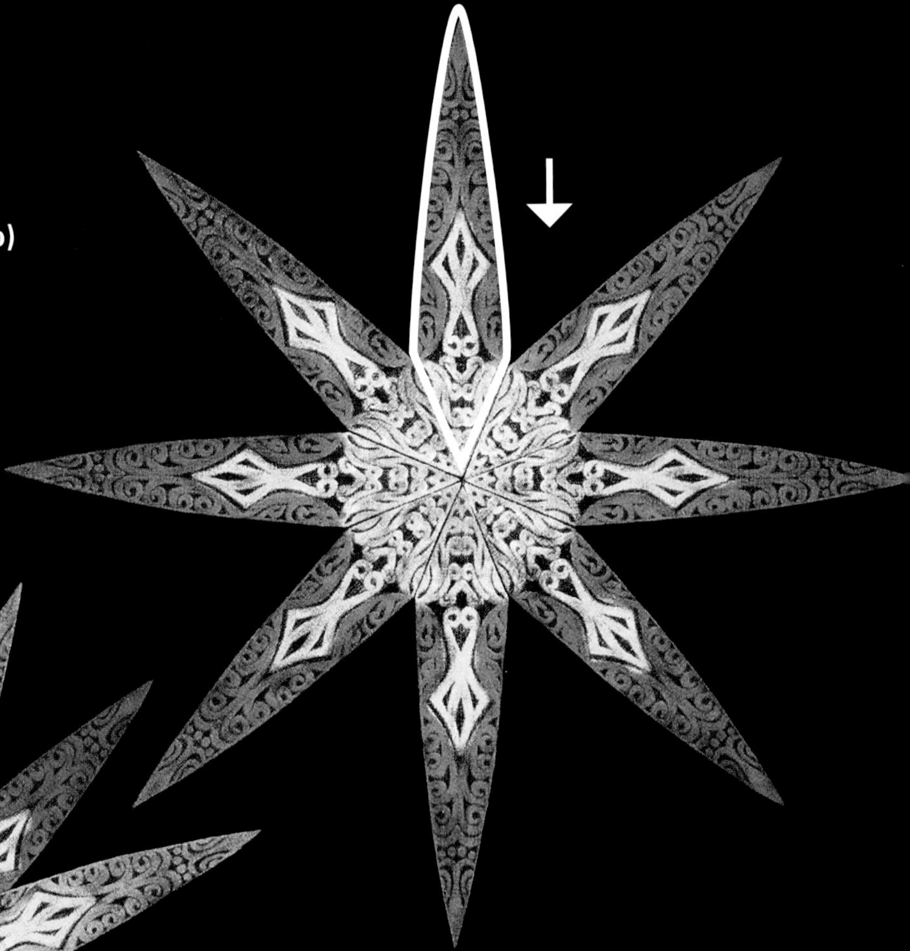

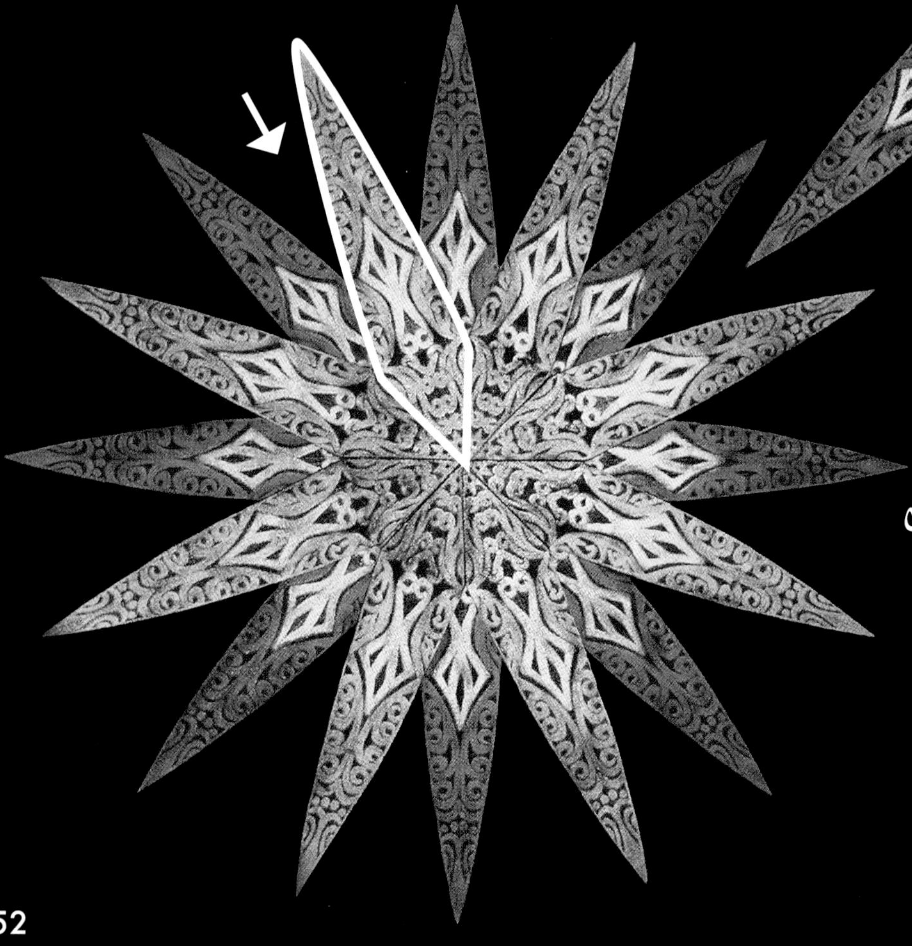

step 2

Shapes required
8 large petals (b)

Diameter: **15"**

52

3

Shapes required:
16 diamonds
8 small Vs

Diameter: **15″**

step

4

Shapes required:
16 small petals
Diameter: **15″**

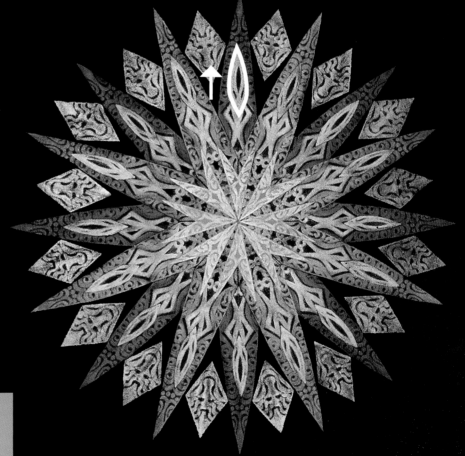

Ursa Minor:

Iridescent – blue, gold, light gold,
purple, red, turquoise

53

Auriga

This star requires 12 orientation points and uses four shapes. You will need:

12 small Vs

12 small petals

6 leaves

6 kites

Step

1

Shapes required:
12 small Vs
Diameter: 5"

Step

2

Shapes required
12 small petals
Diameter: 5"

Auriga Colors:

Iridescent – gold, light gold, turquoise, purple   **Matt** – napthol red

54

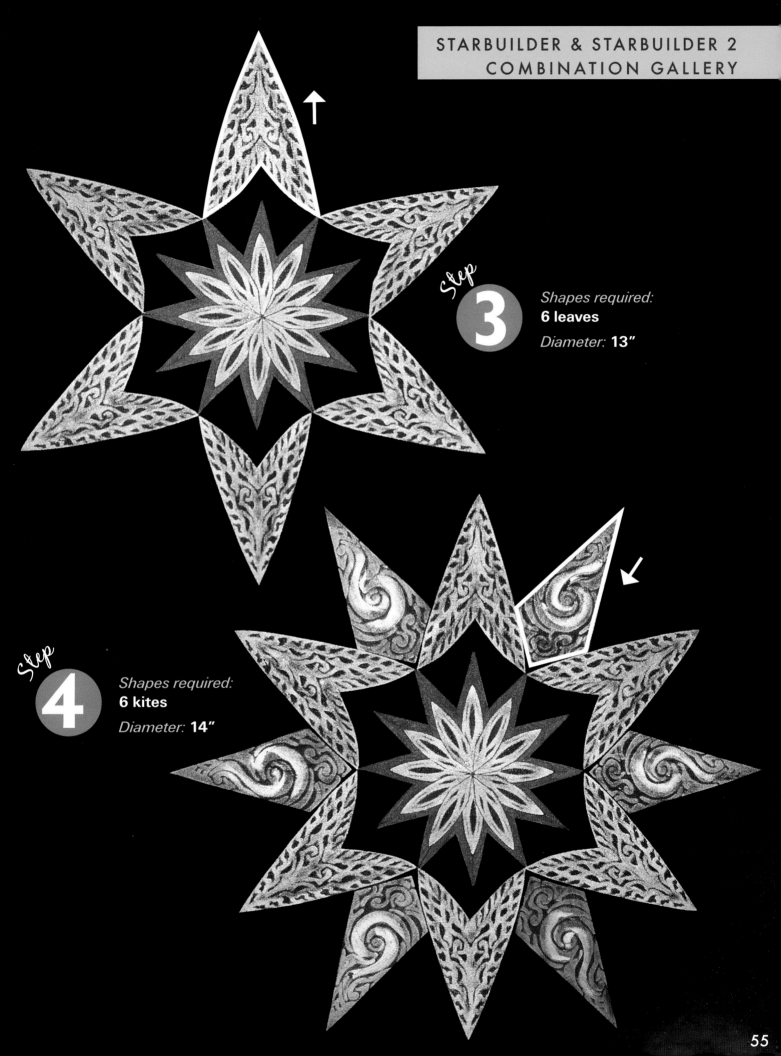

step
3

Shapes required:
6 leaves

Diameter: **13″**

step
4

Shapes required:
6 kites

Diameter: **14″**

Aquila

This star requires 16 orientation points and uses four shapes. You will need:

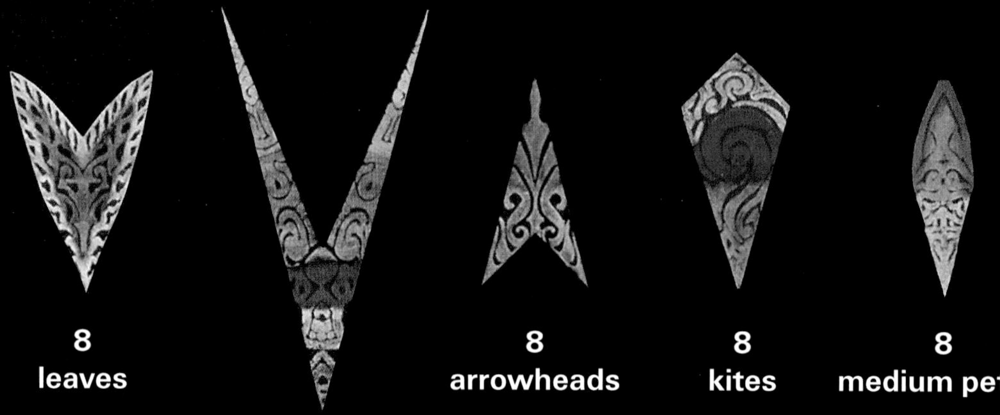

8 leaves

8 big Vs

8 arrowheads

8 kites

8 medium petals

step

1

Shapes required:
8 leaves

Diameter: **9"**

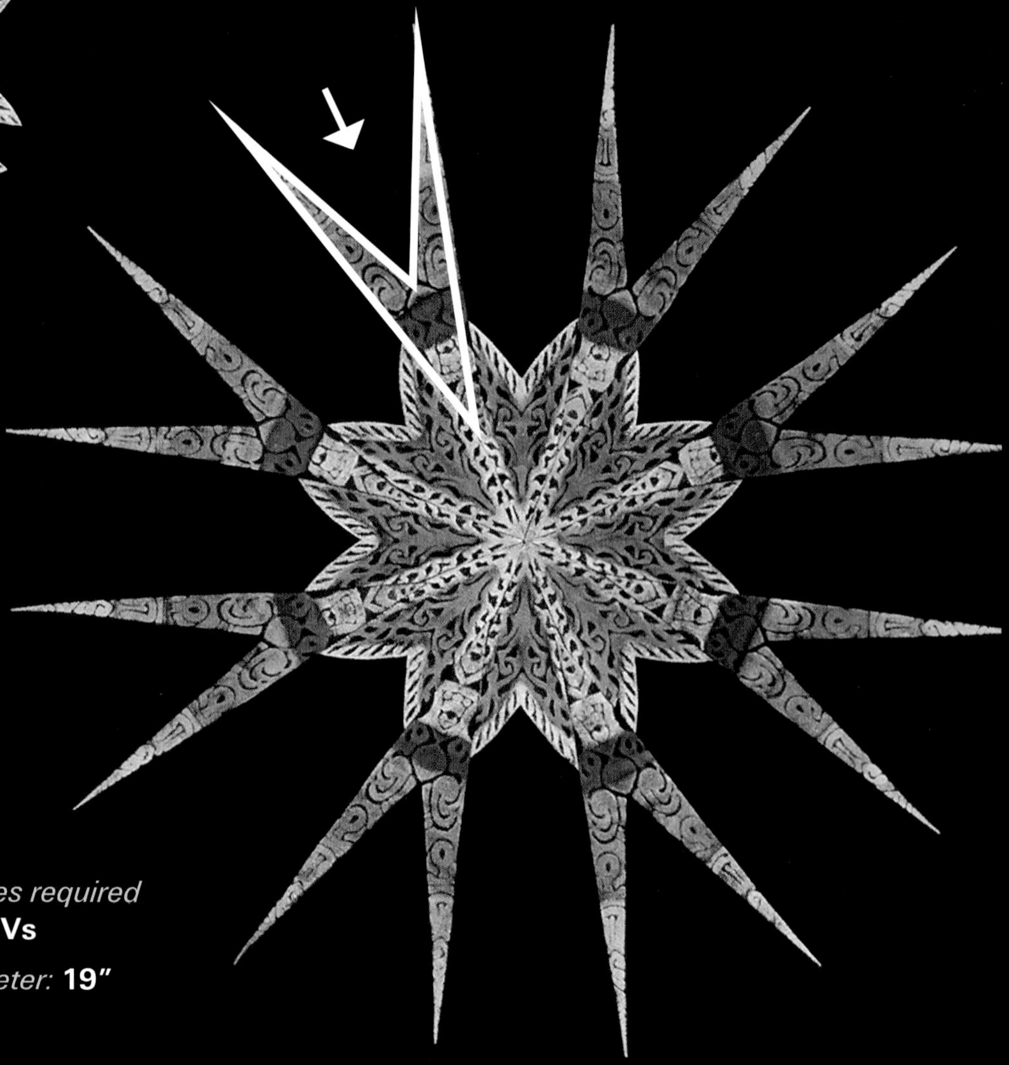

step

2

Shapes required
8 big Vs

Diameter: **19"**

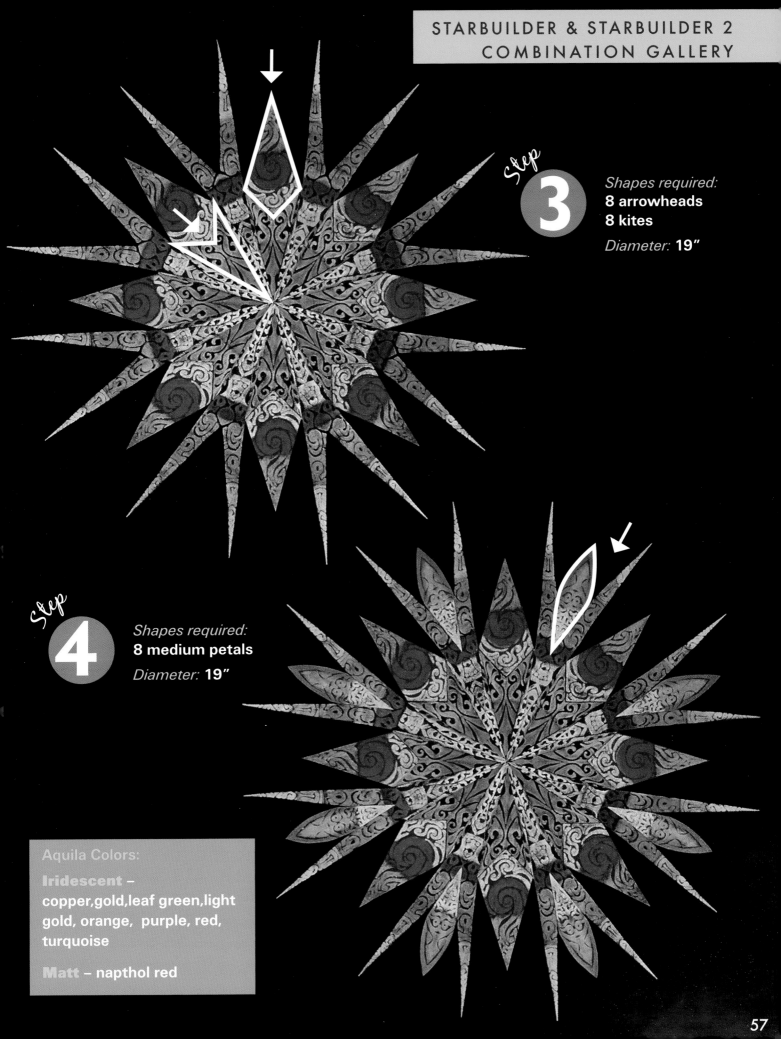

step

3

Shapes required:
8 arrowheads
8 kites

Diameter: **19"**

step

4

Shapes required:
8 medium petals

Diameter: **19"**

Aquila Colors:

Iridescent –
copper,gold,leaf green,light gold, orange, purple, red, turquoise

Matt – napthol red

Dorado

This star requires 10 orientation points and uses five shapes. You will need:

5 large petals

5 kites

5 leaves

5 arrowheads

10 neckties

step **1**

Shapes required:
5 kites

Diameter: **9"**

step **2**

Shapes required
5 leaves

Diameter: **9"**

step
3

Shapes required:
5 large petals
5 arrowheads

Diameter: **17"**

step
4

Shapes required:
10 neckties

Diameter: **17"**

Dorado Colors:

Iridescent – copper, gold, leaf green, light gold, orange, purple, turquoise

Lyra

This star requires 16 orientation points and uses five shapes. You will need:

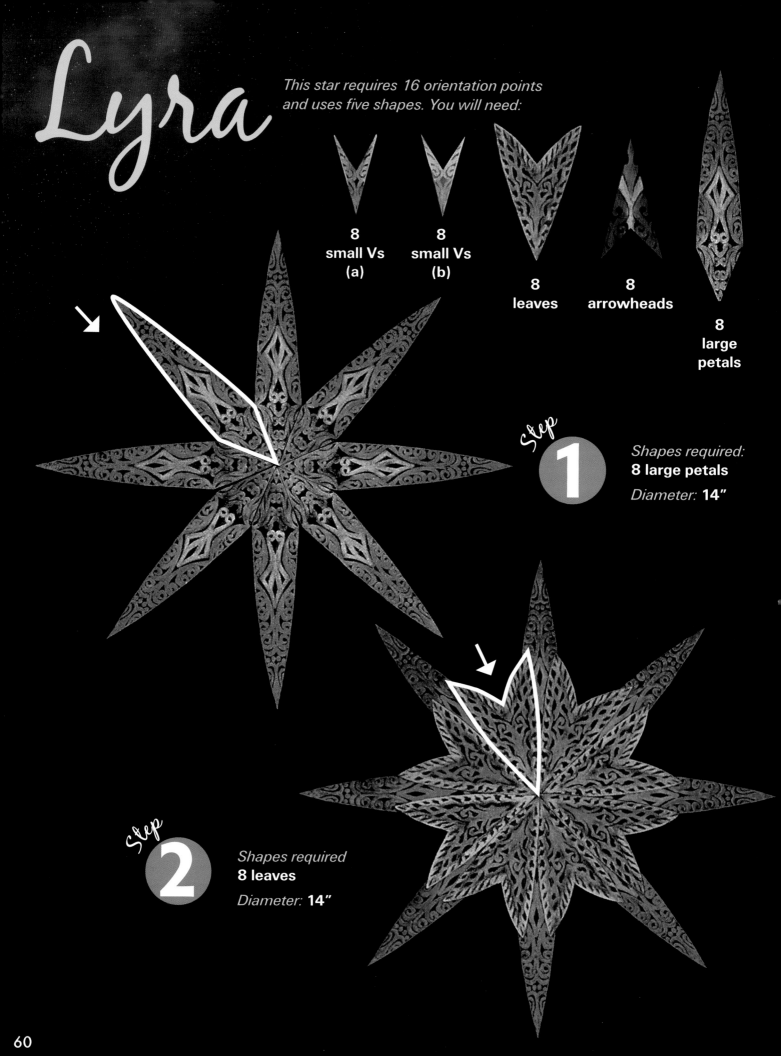

8
small Vs
(a)

8
small Vs
(b)

8
leaves

8
arrowheads

8
large
petals

step 1

Shapes required:
8 large petals
Diameter: **14"**

step 2

Shapes required
8 leaves
Diameter: **14"**

Step

3

Shapes required:
8 arrowheads

Diameter: **14"**

Step

4

Shapes required:
8 small Vs (a)
8 small Vs (b)

Diameter: **14"**

Lyra Colors:

Iridescent – blue, gold, leaf green, light gold, pink, purple, red, turquoise

Pavo

This star requires 8 orientation points and uses seven shapes. You will need:

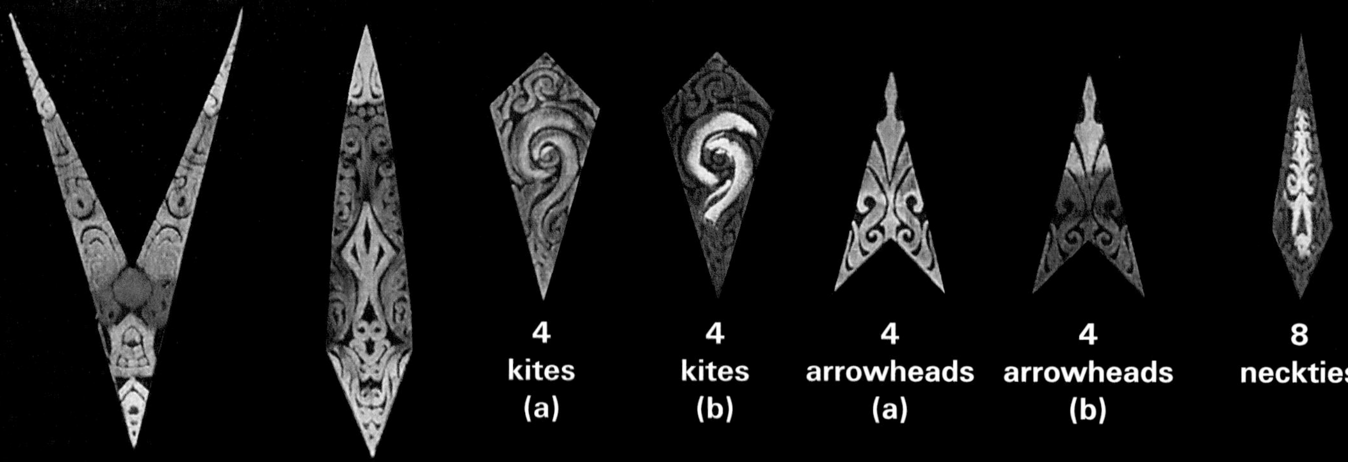

**4
kites
(a)**

**4
kites
(b)**

**4
arrowheads
(a)**

**4
arrowheads
(b)**

**8
neckties**

**4
large Vs**

**4
large petals**

step **1**

Shapes required:
4 kites (a)

Diameter: **8"**

step **2**

Shapes required
4 large Vs
4 kites (a)

Diameter: **15"**

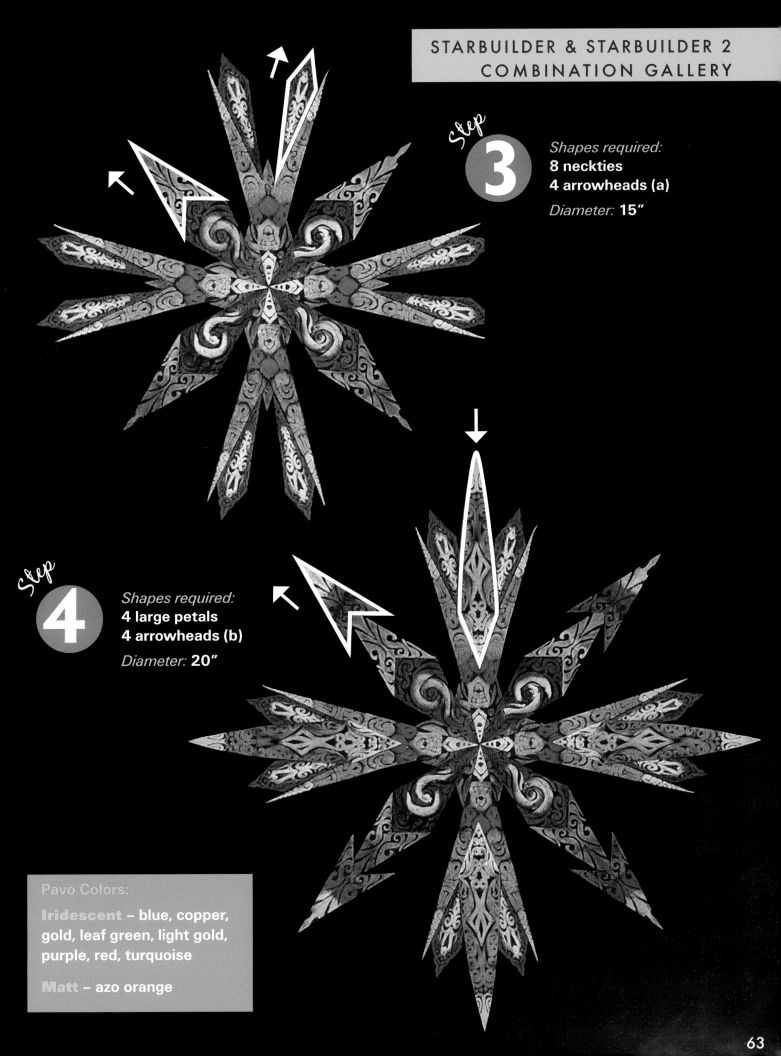

step
3

Shapes required:
**8 neckties
4 arrowheads (a)**

Diameter: **15"**

step
4

Shapes required:
**4 large petals
4 arrowheads (b)**

Diameter: **20"**

Pavo Colors:

Iridescent – **blue, copper,
gold, leaf green, light gold,
purple, red, turquoise**

Matt – **azo orange**

Taurus

This star requires 24 orientation points and uses four shapes. You will need:

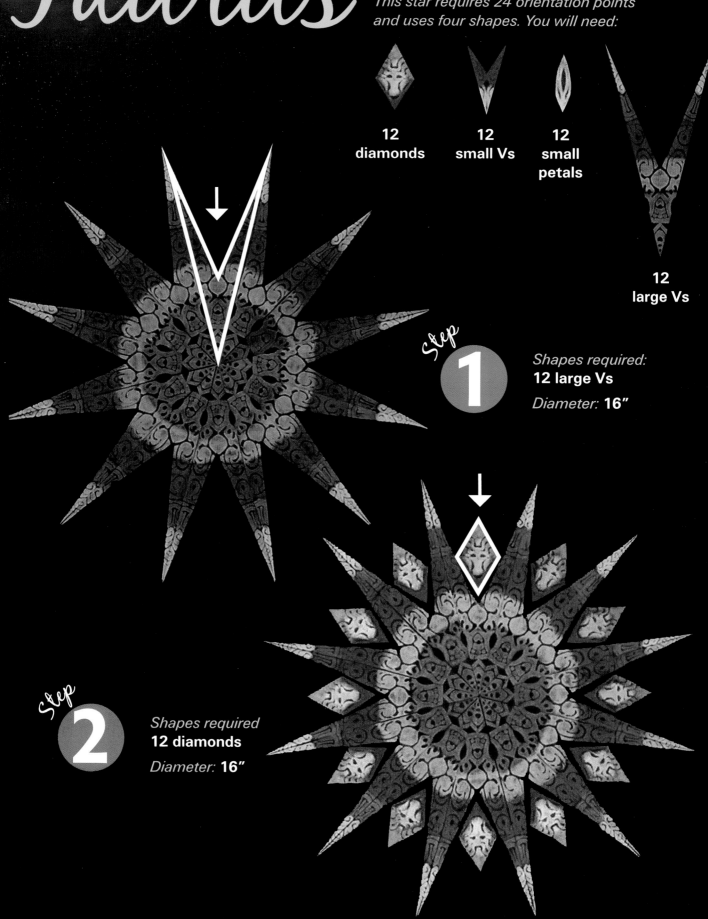

12 diamonds

12 small Vs

12 small petals

12 large Vs

Step 1

Shapes required:
12 large Vs
Diameter: **16"**

Step 2

Shapes required
12 diamonds
Diameter: **16"**

step
3

Shapes required:
12 small Vs
Diameter: **16"**

step
4

Shapes required:
12 small petals
Diameter: **16"**

Taurus Colors:

Iridescent – blue, gold, light gold, orange, purple, red, turquoise

Matt – napthol red

Shapeshifters

Shapes can be cut into sections to **create new shapes** for additional design possibilities.

Arrowhead

Iridescent – gold, turquoise

Matt – napthol red

Cut into three sections along etched lines

Left and Right Twirls
Shapes required:
12 for each star which rotate in opposite directions
Diameter: **4"**

13 Center Shapes
Shapes required: **13**
Diameter: **6"**

Border
Shapes required: **6**
Length: **19"**

Kite

Iridescent – gold, purple, turquoise

Cut into three sections along etched lines

7 Shapes

Shapes required: **7**

Diameter: **5"**

10 Shapes

Shapes required: **10**

Diameter: **4"**

Border 1

Shapes required: **6**   *Length:* **13"**

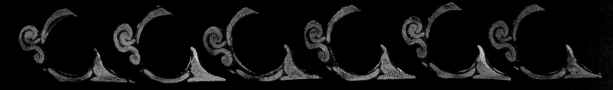

Border 2

Shapes required: **6**   *Length:* **14"**

Medium Petal

Iridescent – orange, purple, turquoise

Cut into two sections along etched lines

Step 1 **Epsilon**
Shapes required: **8**
Diameter: **7"**

Step 2 **Epsilon**
Shapes required: **8**
Diameter: **7"**

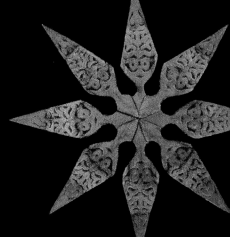

Epsilon
Flip shapes for variations

Border
Shapes required: **8**   *Length:* **18"**

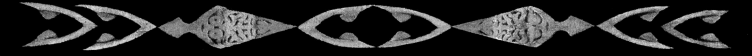

Large Petal

Iridescent – blue, green, light gold, orange, pink, red

Cut into two sections along etched lines. See how many other possibilities you can discover in this large shape!

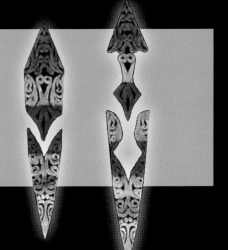

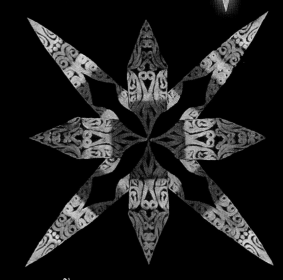

step **1** Beta
Shapes required: **4**

Diameter: **13"**

step **2** Beta
Shapes required: **4**

Diameter: **13"**

Gamma

Shapes required: **7**

Diameter: **9"**

Border

Shapes required: **4**   *Length:* **17"**

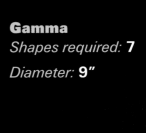

Fish

Angel

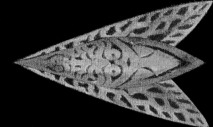

step 1 *Shapes required:*
1 leaf

step 2 *Shapes required:*
1 medium petal

step 3 *Shapes required:*
1 necktie

step 4 *Shapes required:*
3 small petals

Nemo

step 1 *Shapes required:*
2 leaves

step 2 *Shapes required:*
1 large petal

Oscar

Iridescent – blue, gold, leaf green, light gold, purple, turquoise

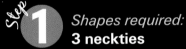

Shapes required:
3 neckties

Shapes required:
**1 arrowhead
cut in half lengthwise**

Shapes required:
1 arrowhead

Shapes required:
**1 arrowhead
cut in half lengthwise**

Birds

Midas

step **1**

Shapes required:
1 leaf

step **2**

Shapes required:
1 arrowhead

step **3**

Shapes required:
1 medium petal

step **4**

Shapes required:
2 neckties

Calypso

step **1**

Shapes required:
3 neckties

step **2**

Shapes required:
1 arrowhead

step **3**

Shapes required:
**1 arrowhead
cut in half lengthwise**

Nosegays

Iridescent –blue, leaf green, light gold, gold, orange, purple, turquoise

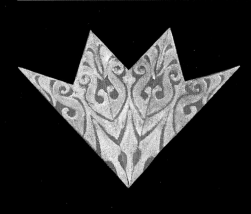

 1

Shapes required:
3 arrowheads

 2

Shapes required:
2 arrowheads

 3

Shapes required:
3 small petals

 4

Shapes required:
1 arrowhead

*Create variations by using the leaf
or necktie shape in step 2.*

Sedona Sunrise
by Laura Murray, quilted by Mary Brandt

Tuscan Sunset
by Laura Murray, quilted by Mary Brandt

Sailor's Compass
by Mary Brandt

Center StarBuilder surrounded by
handpieced Mariner's Compass stars.

Pillow
by Laura Murray

Black Jean Jacket
embellished by Laura Murray

Blue Jean Jacket
embellished by Laura Murray

Jacket
by Lou Scanlon

Pattern is "Pacific Rim" by Lorraine Torrence.

Constellation I
by Laura Murray

Constellation II
by Laura Murray

Star is Born
by Laura Murray

Holiday Stars
by Laura Murray

Stars fused to a
stiff interfacing

**Fantasy Flower I
and II**
*by Laura Murray,
quilted by Mary Brandt*

About Laura

Laura Murray is an artist, entrepreneur, teacher, and author. She is known for her wearable art, which features over-dyed kimono fabrics. Laura's work has appeared in books, magazines, and quilt calendars.

Her quilts have been exhibited internationally in major quilt shows and galleries and have won numerous awards, including Best Wall Quilt from the American Quilters Society in Paducah, Kentucky, and First Place in the Houston International Quilt Festival.

Laura lives with her husband in Minneapolis, Minnesota. She began her experimentation with color and texture in 1989. She left the corporate world in 2000, and founded Laura Murray Designs as a venue to sell her over-dyed kimono fabrics, handmade buttons, and designer garment patterns. Laura's passion for surface design soon resulted in the creation of a stencil collection that featured her favorite images for use with fabric paint and foils. Several years ago, she began exploring Paintstik applications, which led to designing the StarBuilder stamps. These novel stamps filled a missing niche in the tools available to the quilt makers who want to use Paintstiks in new and innovative ways.

Available from
LauraMurrayDesigns.com

Paintstiks and accessories
book, DVD, rubbing plates, no-slip mats, brushes

StarBuilder book, stamps

Foils and accessories
sampler sets, adhesive, and DVD

Art to Wear patterns, one-of-a-kind fabrics, and buttons

Art stencils